WHAT ON EARTH IS A
BUSTARD

?

JENNY TESAR

 A BLACKBIRCH PRESS BOOK
WOODBRIDGE, CONNECTICUT

Published by Blackbirch Press, Inc.
260 Amity Road
Woodbridge, Connecticut 06525

©1997 Blackbirch Press, Inc.
First Edition

Printed in the United States of America

10 9 8 7 6 5 4 3 2

Photo Credits

Cover, title page: ©Tom McHugh/Photo Researchers, Inc.
Pages 4—5: ©Zig Leszczynski/Animals Animals; page 6: ©R. Van Nostrand/Photo
Researchers, Inc.; page 9: ©Gunter Ziesler/Peter Arnold, Inc.; page 10: ©Fran
Allan/Animals Animals; page 12: ©Anup and Mahoj Shah/Animals Animals; page 13:
©Anup and Mahoj Shah/Animals Animals; page 15: ©M. P. Kahl/Photo Researchers, Inc.;
pages 16—17: ©Joe McDonald/Animals Animals; page 16 (inset): ©John Gerlach/Animals
Animals; pages 18—19: ©Anup and Mahoj Shah/Animals Animals; page 19 (inset): ©Arthur
Gloor/Animals Animals; page 21: ©Len Rue, Jr./Animals Animals; page 22: ©Fritz
Pölking/Peter Arnold, Inc.; page 24: ©Michael Dick/Animals Animals; page 25: ©P. & W.
Ward/Oxford Scientific Films/Animals Animals; pages 26—27: ©Norman R.
Lightfoot/Photo Researchers, Inc.; page 29: ©Stan Osolinski/Oxford Scientific
Films/Animals Animals.

Library of Congress Cataloging-in-Publication Data

Tesar, Jenny E.
What on earth is a bustard? / by Jenny Tesar. — 1st edition.
   p.   cm. — (What on earth series)
   Includes bibliographical references and index.
Summary: Identifies physical characteristics, lifestyle, habitat, reproductive process, and
methods of survival of this bird as well as environmental issues relating to it.
   ISBN 1-56711-102-5 (lib. bdg. : alk. paper)
   1. Bustards—Juvenile literature. [1. Bustards. 2. Birds.]
I. Title. II. Series.
QL696.G86T47   1997
598.3'1—dc20
                        95-47540
                           CIP
                           AC

What does it look like?

Where does it live?

What does it eat?

How does it reproduce?

How does it survive?

TURN THESE PAGES AND FIND OUT!

The bustard is a plump bird with a long neck and long legs. It lives on the ground in the grasslands of Europe, Africa, Asia, and Australia. It usually moves about by walking or running, but it is also quite a strong flyer.

Scientists have identified 24 kinds, or species, of bustards. Some of these birds are about the size of a chicken. Others are bigger than turkeys. One of the largest species, the great bustard, is the world's heaviest flying bird.

A KORI BUSTARD WALKS THROUGH ITS GRASSY AFRICAN HABITAT.

Bustards have been classified by scientists as belonging to the bird family Otididae (or Otidae). The name is based on Greek words that mean "family with long ear feathers." The adult males of most species have a plume of long feathers on each side of the head or neck.

People in England were the first to call these birds *bustards*, a name that has been used for more than 500 years. It seems to have been based on two Latin words that translate as "slow bird." This makes sense because bustards fly more slowly than most other kinds of birds do.

A MALE EASTERN GREAT
BUSTARD DISPLAYS SOME OF
HIS IMPRESSIVE FEATHERS.

Small species, such as the crested bustard, lesser florican, and pygmy bustard, are less than 15 inches (38 centimeters) tall and weigh less than 3 pounds (1.4 kilograms). The great bustard and the kori are the largest species. A male great bustard may be 43 inches (110 centimeters) tall and weigh more than 40 pounds (18 kilograms)!

In many species, males are larger and heavier than females. A male great bustard may weigh four times as much as a female.

The sexes also have different plumage, or coats of feathers. The males of most bustard species have more striking colors and patterns than the females. Males also have long plumes or other fancy feathers on their head or neck.

Bustards do not sing songs, but some of them have loud calls. For example, the Senegal bustard of Africa loudly calls "oo-warka! oo-warka!" The kori calls "kah! kah! kah!" And the buff-crested bustard actually whistles!

A BLACK BUSTARD CALLS OUT FROM ITS HOME IN NAMIBIA, AFRICA.

A BUSTARD'S WINGS ARE LONG, BROAD, AND POWERFUL.

A bustard's wings are fairly long and broad. This shape gives the bustard the power it needs for a fast takeoff. Once in the air, the bustard flies by flapping its wings. As it flies, it keeps its head and neck straight out in front.

A bustard's legs are long and strong. Unlike humans, bustards—and almost every other kind of bird—do not stand on the flat of their feet. They stand on their toes. A bustard's foot has three short, strong toes that point forward. Like many other running birds, bustards do not have a hind toe. The claws at the end of the toes grow throughout a bustard's life but never get very long. They are worn down during walking, digging for food, and other activities.

Most bustards are found in dry, warm environments. They live in wide, open areas with tall grasses and very few trees. Some live in semideserts, which are dry areas with some grasses and shrubs. Bustards spend most of their time on the ground, living in small groups of about a dozen birds.

A BLACK-BELLIED BUSTARD IN A GRASSLAND.

TWO KORI BUSTARDS ROAM THEIR SHRUB-FILLED HABITAT.

Bustards spend much of the day walking around in search of food. They depend on their heavy bills to pick up and hold the things they catch. Most of the food is snapped up from the ground or removed from plants, but sometimes a bustard uses its bill to dig into the soil for a tasty morsel. Like all birds, bustards are toothless and swallow their food whole.

Bustards eat both plants and animals. They eat seeds, flowers, berries, leaves, and other plant parts. They also eat mice, lizards, baby birds, and other small animals. And they are great insect hunters, catching and eating huge numbers of grasshoppers and locusts. This makes them a welcome sight to farmers, especially in Africa, where grasshoppers and locusts are serious pests that destroy valuable crops.

A BUSTARD'S BILL IS LONG AND STRONG, DESIGNED TO PICK UP AND HOLD FOOD.

BUSTARDS WANDER AMONG A HERD OF WILDEBEEST.
INSET: A BURCHELL'S ZEBRA

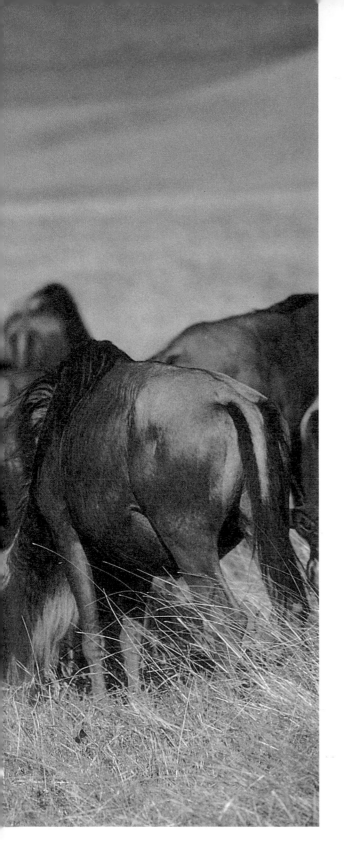

There is an abundance of life on the grasslands where bustards roam. On the African grasslands, for example, there are lions, giraffes, wildebeests, zebras, and hyenas. There are also many other birds, such as ostriches, eagles, vultures, and hornbills. Hiding among the grasses are mice, insects, and other small creatures.

On the Australian grasslands, bustards share their habitats with animals such as kangaroos. There are large colorful flocks of parrots and parakeets. Wedge-tailed eagles watch for mice, rabbits, and other prey.

Some of the other animals that live in the grasslands prey on bustards. Wild cats and birds of prey, such as eagles and hawks, attack and eat small bustards in Africa and Asia. Also, many bustard eggs and chicks are eaten by wild cats, mongooses, hyenas, and other predators. Wild dogs attack the Australian bustards and also eat their eggs.

LIONS AND OTHER WILD CATS POSE A CONSTANT DANGER TO BUSTARDS IN AFRICA.

HYENAS AND WILD DOGS ARE COMMON PREDATORS OF BUSTARDS.

Bustards have useful defenses for survival. Most important, they can speedily outrun many enemies. As they run, they keep looking back over their shoulders. If an enemy gets too close, a bustard flies up into the air.

Camouflage is important to bustards. Their feathers blend in well with their surroundings, which makes it almost impossible for enemies to see them. This is quite an achievement for such a large bird!

Sometimes bustards crouch down and hide among the grasses. A bustard will sleep close to the ground, too, pulling in its head so that it rests between the shoulders.

ONE OF A BUSTARD'S BEST DEFENSES IS CAMOUFLAGE, HIDING BY BLENDING IN WITH THE SURROUNDINGS.

When spring comes to the grasslands, each male bustard establishes a territory, which he guards from other male bustards. The territory is an area where the male can attract and mate with a female.

Male bustards use spectacular displays to attract a female. They fluff out and shake their feathers, twist their wings, and inflate a pouch in their throats. They also leap into the air, parade around, and pose like movie stars.

After the female responds to a male's courtship dance, the two birds mate. During mating, the male fertilizes the eggs inside the female. The fertilized eggs eventually develop into baby bustards.

A MALE KORI BUSTARD PUFFS OUT
HIS FEATHERS IN A DRAMATIC
MATING DISPLAY.

BUSTARD EGGS ARE LAID IN SHALLOW HOLES OR PROTECTED AREAS ON THE GROUND.

Following mating, the female bustard lays the eggs in a shallow hole on the ground, perhaps under a bush or in tall grass. One to five speckled eggs are laid in the hole. Each egg has a hard shell that protects the developing baby. The female then sits on and incubates the eggs; that is, she keeps the eggs warm so they will hatch. In some bustard species, the males and females take turns incubating the eggs.

BOTH MALES AND FEMALES WORK TO KEEP THEIR EGGS WARM.

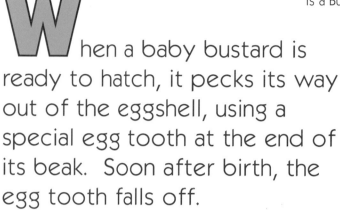

When a baby bustard is ready to hatch, it pecks its way out of the eggshell, using a special egg tooth at the end of its beak. Soon after birth, the egg tooth falls off.

Newborn bustards are well developed. They have speckled feathers and are soon ready to leave the nest. Even though they are able to fly when they are only five to six weeks old, they stay with their mother until they are several months old. At first, the mother brings her young food to eat. Later, they follow her about and learn how to find and catch food on their own.

Some bustards have relatively long life spans, compared to other birds. Larger species can live to be more than 30 years old.

A YOUNG WHITE-BELLIED BUSTARD
FOLLOWS ITS MOTHER THROUGH
TALL GRASSES IN KENYA, AFRICA.

Because of human activities, bustards are now rare in many places where they once were plentiful. Some species are even in danger of becoming extinct.

People have settled in grasslands where bustards once roamed. They have built towns and roads and have replaced native grasses with fields of corn, wheat, and other crops. These actions have ruined the bustards' habitats and have disturbed the natural balance of the region. Chemical fertilizers and insecticides have killed bustards and destroyed their eggs. People also hunt bustards, killing them for food and sport.

It would be sad if Earth were to lose the many varieties of bustards. These handsome birds are fascinating to watch, especially during mating season. They play an important role in their environment, and, because they eat large numbers of grasshoppers and other pests, they are very valuable to humans.

A BLACK-BELLIED BUSTARD CALLS OUT WITH ITS LOUD VOICE.

Glossary

bustard pronunciation: buss • terd

camouflage Blending in with the surroundings; used to hide from enemies.

extinct No longer in existence.

fertilization The joining of a male sex cell, called a sperm, and a female sex cell, called an egg. Fertilization is a part of reproduction.

fertilizer A substance used to improve soil so that plants will grow better.

habitat The place where an organism lives.

incubation To sit on fertilized eggs and keep them warm so that babies will develop and hatch.

insecticide A chemical used to kill insects.

plumage The coat of feathers that covers a bird.

prey To hunt other animals; animals that are hunted.

species A group of living things that are closely related to one another. Members of a species can reproduce with one another.

territory An area that is occupied and defended by an animal.

Further Reading

Brooks, F. *Protecting Endangered Species*. Tulsa,
   OK: EDC Publishing, 1991.

Chinery, Michael. *Grassland Animals*. New York:
   Random House Books for Young Readers, 1992.

Ganeri, Anita. *Birds*. New York: Watts, 1992.

Gray, Ian. *Birds of Prey*. New York: Watts, 1991.

Losito, Linda. *Birds: Aerial Hunters*. New York:
   Facts On File, 1989.

Parry-Jones, Jemima. *Amazing Birds of Prey*. New
   York: Knopf Books for Young Readers, 1999.

Ricciuti, Edward R. *Birds*. Woodbridge, CT:
   Blackbirch Press, Inc., 1993.

Sabin, Louis. *Grasslands*. Mahwah, NJ: Troll
   Associates, 1985.

Stanley-Baker, Penny. *Australia: On the Other Side
   of the World*. Ossining, NY: Young Discovery
   Library, 1988.

Stewart, Frances T. and Charles P. *Birds and Their
   Environments*. New York: HarperCollins, 1988.

Index